GOD'S
Poetic Moments Within

CATHERINE M. BURNS

ISBN 978-1-0980-2226-6 (paperback)
ISBN 978-1-0980-2227-3 (digital)

Christian Faith Publishing, Inc.
832 Park Avenue
Meadville, PA 16335
www.christianfaithpublishing.com

Printed in the United States of America

Contents

Preface

I believe that every person has a God given gift. I refer to it as a person's passion, something that comes easy to them and they enjoy doing at the same time. When I was young I heard the saying "Do what you love and you will be rich." As I thought about this saying, I could think of a lot of things I liked, but what did I really deeply love? This was a question I asked myself throughout life.

One evening as I lie in bed saying my prayers, I asked God to reveal my passion to me. I prayed he would show me what I was made to do. Suddenly, I heard a voice within. It told me to look next to my bed. A nightstand was there.

I opened the nightstand door and looked inside. I saw books I had read, magazines, bookmarks and a folder. The folder had poetry, short stories and writings I had compiled over the years.

I do love to write, I thought. I have found myself at times rushing home going directly to my computer to get my thoughts on paper before I lost the words I had in my heart. Maybe this was my passion? As I thought about this, I suddenly felt peace within. It felt right, it felt like me. This is what I loved to do. I just never thought of it as my passion. I considered it a hobby.

I remembered two readings in the New Testament. The first reading, Matthew 25:14–30, was I guilty of putting my talents in a box and burying them? Why didn't I see this sooner? I just never thought of my writings in that way before. I was thankful to God for showing me this truth.

Was I the seed that fell among thorns in Luke 8:4–15? Did I get so caught up in the worries and riches of this world that I did not see what was right in front of me all these years? Well, if so I needed to now become the seed that fell on good soil. I need to bear fruit with what God has given me.

With this thought in mind, I went through my writing folder, as raggedy and worn out it was from over the years. I picked out 5 of my favorite poems and compiled them together in this book. These poems meant a lot to me since they dealt with my thoughts and feelings for that time in my life. I said yes to God. If this is what he wanted me to do then he would make a way. I asked him to take me out of my comfort zone and help me move forward. I decided to have the attitude of Jesus' mother Mary and say yes to God and his plans for my life. As you read this book, I hope it will help you discover your passion and trust the Lord wherever he may lead you!

When I was young, I pictured God as a large serious man sitting on his mighty throne in the heavens. I saw him as observing us here below on earth as we live our lives. I didn't feel a personal relationship with him as a loving God. To me, he was more of a disciplinarian watching from a distance. I felt that God had ultimate power and was someone to be feared rather than loved.

As I aged and became a young adult, I realized how wrong I was. God intervened in my life, and I realized that all the years of hearing "Jesus loves you" were true. It took a low point in my life to cause me to look up and see what he did out of love for us on the cross. God's love, his son, on display for all to see. Jesus, with his arms wide open and welcoming as they always will be.

That same love and comfort are there for you also. Remember, you are not alone for he cares.

"Behold the rainbow! Then bless
its maker" Sirach 43:11

He Cares

I used to think God didn't care,
Upon his high throne, sitting there,
Looking down with an angry brow,
Watching for calamity among the crowd,
Only then to intervene, and cause a catastrophic scene.

A judging God is all I knew,
"He doesn't care that much for you,"
In my head a voice would say,
As I lived my life, from day to day.

Then troubles came as they always do,
No one found that I could look to,
Deep loneliness is all I felt,
The cards of life I had been dealt.

For who am I but a grain of sand,
Falling helplessly through his hand,
There was no where that I could turn,
A way of life I had come to learn.

I lowered my head and looked above,
Inside my heart I felt his love,
God let me know from deep within,
He sent his son to carry my sin.

As small in this universe I must be,
It is amazing how much he cares for me,
It does not matter where I've been,
Every part of my life matters to him.

God loves me more than I could know,
I felt it, I know it, he told me so,
A loving Father for all my life,
Who understands and knows my strife.
For all my life God is a part,
I am never alone, since he lives in my heart.

When a parent loses an unborn baby, the pain is real. I experienced this firsthand when my brother and sister-in-law had a miscarriage. They were so sad. My sister-in-law lay on the couch and cried for days. There was no consoling her. They not only lost a baby, they also lost the unspoken future hopes, dreams, and plans that were held deep inside their hearts. The future they imagined was suddenly and swiftly gone forever. It was a devastating loss and painful to watch.

Though there is so much sadness with losing an unborn child, we also have hope when we know Christ. He will let us understand that one day we will be with our precious child again. The sweet unseen face along with the unique personality of our child will be revealed when we meet again, and oh, what a reunion that shall be!

Baby of Mine

Though you never saw me,
In secret I did grow.
A joyous mystery of love,
Oh how were we to know?

Happiness we did not share,
Days we never had,
Our future dreams are only thoughts,
Our hearts, broken and sad.

My Daddy's nose, your big brown eyes,
The face you could not see.
Dear Mom, please know that all is well,
Our Lord now cares for me.

Together we will be one day,
For now we are apart.
Please try to understand and know,
Your love lives in my heart.

E ach part of our body has been assigned a special task. Good or bad, our hand was made to give action to our thoughts. The power to give, take, help, harm, hold, or release have been granted to our hand. Our heart, controlling our thoughts, is the true director of our hand. Knowing that, I look at my hand and pray for God's guidance over my heart. I pray that my heartfelt thoughts will direct my hand to do the work that is pleasing to him. Laying my heart in God's hands with trust, I look forward to the task he has set before me. May my hand do what God has created it for, only then will the heart be filled with peace and joy!

My Hand

I look at my hand and what do I see?
An instrument God has given to me,
I look at my hand and what do I know?
My heart will decide which way it will go.

May it always be to help and aid,
Never to hurt or push away,
Let its touch be gentle and kind,
A helping hand for all to find.

My hand shall grow and change with time,
The journey for God to guide along,
My Lord will strengthen and shape the heart,
Together for life, they will grow strong.

And when the day is extra long,
I pray for my hand to be extra strong.
Always ready to give some more,
For this is the task my hand was made for.

A wonderful moment in ones life is becoming a parent. When looking upon your babies sweet little face, you will instantly fall in a different kind of love, a love that can only be described as "baby love.". That baby love will change your life forever in the most amazing ways.

I remember when I held my baby for the very first time. I was unexpectedly overcome with emotion. I asked God, just this one time, could he please let time stand still so I could stay here a little longer? I didn't want this moment to end. I had found my happy place.

As life and time move on, as they always will, I found joy in every new step. Looking back, I have memories that take me back to that happy place that I will cherish for a lifetime.

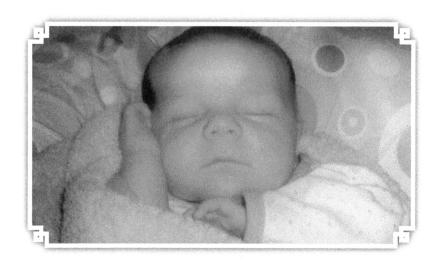

Baby Love

I remember when I saw you,
Wishing how time would stay,
Frozen, as my arms embraced you,
Could forever be today?

I remember pure and lovely,
Tiny eyes that searched my face,
The beginning of our journey,
How I loved this happy place.

I remember the excitement,
Joy with every little feat,
How I thrilled to see the changes,
Baby days so soft and sweet.

I remember, though time passes,
Fairy tales and nursery rhymes,
Yesterdays treasured memories,
In my heart the best of times.

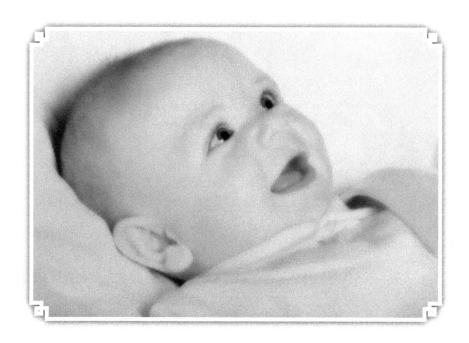

I remember the very first time I saw my newborn baby. I looked into my little one's eyes and saw so much more than just a sweet face. I could see that there was a whole new world awaiting both of us. I knew that deep inside, come what may, I was in this journey for a lifetime. It was a journey that would be filled with hope, joy, anticipation, wonder, and some fear of the unknown. More than anything else there was an overwhelming feeling of love. Love that would give me the strength I needed for the future task ahead.

I was keenly aware of the enormous responsibility I was given as a parent to guide this new life. I humbly asked God for help with the task he had set before me. With a forever faithful and thankful heart, I now move forward. A truth I have come to learn is that the best future for my baby lies in the future God has already planned. It is my desire to know and follow God's plans so that this little one can be all that they were created for.

A Mother's Journey

A Mother looks upon her child,
Their eyes lock as if one.
Though she sees more than a child,
Two lives have just begun.

Where shall we go? Who shall you be?
New adventures to be revealed,
Like an envelope opening to the world,
A secret life is now unsealed.

Whatever the journey, whomever the child,
A gift of life faithfully given.
A unique and precious heart to be guided,
Created to be loved and fully livin.

Time ticks on as it always will,
A hidden personality begins to show,
Like a flower blooming for the first time,
A rainbow of colors starts to grow.

Lord, all I ask is to fulfill the task,
You have entrusted for me to do,
When all is said and the day is done,
May this little one grow to please you.

About the Author

Catherine M. Burns was born in Bedford, Ohio, and since the age of 6 years old has resided in Weirton, West Virginia, a small steel town outside of Pittsburgh, Pennsylvania, for most of her life. She has been writing poetry and short stories for much of her life which express her walk with God through it all. Heeding God's call to share her poetry as a way to give understanding and hope to others in their lifes walk, she compiled a collection of her favorite poems to share.

Being born the second oldest of eight children has the provided experience of sharing, caring, and helping others. She has been married to her husband James for over thirty years. Together they have three sons, Jacob, Justin, and Jonathan, who gave her much inspiration. A registered nurse for over twenty-five years, she currently works in a large Catholic hospital where she is able to care for others with God's guidance. She is a member of St. Paul Catholic Church in Weirton and a member of the Mission Council at her workplace. Mission Council allows God's work in the hospital and community with service projects aiding the poor.

Her personal interests include cooking, reading, crafting, walking, enjoying her sons' sports activities, spending time with friends and family, and taking care of their sweet family dog Chloe.

In her writings, her heart desires to follow what is said in Psalm 102:18: 'Write down for the coming generation what the Lord did, so that people not yet born will praise him.'